The Beekeeper
and other love poems

The Beekeeper
and other love poems

by

Barbara Loots

Cover design by Shay Culligan
Cover photograph by Allison Archer
Author photograph by Alex Treaster

ISBN: 978-1-952326-45-5

Kelsay Books
502 South 1040 East, A-119
American Fork, Utah, 84003

For the beekeeper with all my love

Acknowledgments

The author gratefully acknowledges the following publications in which many of these poems first appeared:

Better Than Starbucks

I-70 Review

Light Poetry Magazine

Lighten Up Online

The Literary Nest

The Lyric

Measure

The Orchards Poetry Journal

Contents

I place my feet with care in such a world.
—William Stafford

I. All That Matters

Let lovers go fresh and sweet to be undone…
— Richard Wilbur

Just Now

The yellow house across the corner
catches the morning sun,
its red-trimmed windows blinking open
to the day begun.

Four squirrels play at aimless chasing
up and down the trees.
Clover spilling over the hillside
waits for the honeybees.

Nothing, nothing in a hurry.
Nowhere to hurry to.
No time but the present moment.
No one but you.

Home Again

We chose the house together with a glance
our eyes exchanged upon the first steps in,
knowing at once the place where lives begin
again was here, through merest happenstance.
We saw its ragged past and took a chance.
We noted damage where the house had been
neglected, sensing underneath the skin
of its old age a story of romance.
Now settled in with books and furniture,
one cat, and two of every pan and pot,
we often smile and wonder how we knew,
how we could be so reckless and so sure,
as every living day unfolds a plot
we cannot guess but simply move into.

The Beekeeper

You understand the bees as someone can
who always has a purpose and a plan,
you who were doubtless destined to become
a brother to that underlying hum
of giving life. Within the teeming hive,
the pure mind of creation seems to thrive
in harmony, with order in the comb
and sweet abundance in a perfect home.

You witness life in stages, each one brief,
driven by instinct, with the sting of grief.
You study the arcane and gentle ways
to please the queen in her productive days.
Drawn to the bees as I am drawn to you,
partner in building up and making new,
you are the keeper of deep mysteries,
invisible as love among the bees.

Moon Landing

Fifty years. I was but twenty-two.
The moon was landed on. I married you

that very day. And all the years thereafter
He promised me the moon, I said. The laughter

enhanced the romance. I was so naïve.
And yet, for decades, managed to believe

moon-smitten, I had found my perfect mate
and sealed the deal on that historic date.

What did I know? The body and the mind
adjust to circumstances. Love is blind.

But now I see, this anniversary year
without you, how my life has lifted clear

of old illusions, and the past is good
for being brave and better understood.

The End

When loving could no longer make you stay,
it did the next best thing and said, *Let go*.

And so we both did. When you went away,
illusion snapped. I was the last to know.

Recycling

With chirps and whistles
like the birds that sing
all summer in the branches,
these dull logs now
catch and quarrel, spit and fling
their last kites to the sideways wind
that rushes up the stack,
that sucks the juice and gives
hot blossoms back.
There sizzle for us
a thousand suns of June
to warm one dreary, snowbound
afternoon.

Another Summer

We seem to assume the island will merely wait
for summer when we return with our loads of gear,
the time of the solstice. Thus we anticipate

the coming again of us for another year
unchanged. Yet nothing stays as it was before,
the paths overgrown, the neighbors no longer here,

the ravel of memories locked by a cottage door,
whatever survived the siege of wind and ice,
whatever a nail or screwdriver might restore.

We settle ourselves, and settle for beans and rice
we left in the cupboard, thankful to celebrate
what hasn't been nibbled away by ants and mice.

The winter comes soon enough. It is not too late
to love what we find for now on the sparsest plate.

All That Matters

Evening hour at Blackwater Lake in August.
Glass half-full of whiskey, and other pleasures,
your cigar smoke drifting in my direction
sweeter than incense.

Lives we left behind will go on without us,
still may be there when we return to claim them.
Meanwhile, all that matters is here between us
silent as sunset.

Baldcypress in Ontario

For Jane

A seedling only eighteen inches tall,
it bravely sprouted several tiny leaves.
And that is how we left it in the fall.

Elsewhere, the widow of a woodsman grieves
who gave us this to plant, his legacy
of thirst for life. Our northern shore receives

the gift for now of hope and memory.
But up here, winter happens dark and deep,
an icy trial for a fragile tree

born in the warmer south. So may it keep
its toehold and revive itself in spring,
roots stubborn even through the long, cold sleep.

There is a time it's said for everything,
whatever chance the elements may bring.

The Train

Touching your face with my two hands at night,
like the last gesture love will ever make,
I sense you slipping, slipping out of sight
into the shadow from which none awake.

I wait for my own sleep, anticipation
fixed on the rumble of a distant train
until it comes rushing, rushing through the station,
mysterious windows flashing in my brain

a lifetime of looking, view after glancing view.
Beside me in the dark, your breathing slows.
And I pray to journey through the night with you,
in this or any sleep the spirit knows.

II. Ars Poetica

The utmost of ambition is to lodge a few poems
where they will be hard to get rid of.

—Robert Frost

Ars Poetica

A reader first, I need to see the notes
and make my fingers find them on the keys.
Watching the way the music almost floats
from hands of virtuosos with pure ease,
I sense my clumsy mind gets in the way
of some electric knowing never taught,
imbedded in the muscles, like ballet,
bypassing effort, repetition, thought.
My plodding practice? Never is it dance.
Yet sometimes elemental joy or rage,
the whole of being, or a lucky chance
enact a pirouette upon the page.
Some music of the spheres I never learned
summons a poem given and not earned.

Loony Tune at Blackwater Lake

It's tempting. Every word that rhymes with loon
hovers in the air this Sunday afternoon.
But it's July. I'll have to give up June.
No matter. Songbirds lend a friendly tune
that mingles with the soft and silky croon
of poplars, wind that fills the white balloon
of sails across the lake. I'm not immune
to romance, love's elaborate cocoon,
yet mind the setting sun, the rising moon
that measure moments hastening toward the fun-
erary endings coming soon. So soon. So soon.

Anthology Hangover in Hendecasyllabics

Sitting down with a cup of warmed-up coffee,
caught the moonrise this morning, waning crescent.
Should not this be a perfect poem moment?

Nothing doing. I'd like to stick with silence.
Birdsong, yes, and the plunk of water lapping.

Rilke pops in to tell me *Space is endless.*
Frost insists I get up and climb those birches.
Meanwhile, Edna Millay's still on the ferry,
back and forth, and I'm seasick with her sighing.

Shut up, poets. I'm done with you. Stop talking.
Let this moon be a Bashō, only wordless.

Language Barrier

Non-conscious but highly intelligent algorithms may soon know us better than we know ourselves.
                                        —Yuval Noah Harari

I think of Hebrew as an ancient tongue
rendered as *thee* and *thine* and *thou shalt not,*
although I realize it thrives among
the living, energetic polyglot
of arguments delivered, ballads sung,
of all persuasions angled into thought
with untranslatable philosophy
beneath the words dividing you from me.

My Latin fades. My French? Not *magnifique.*
Two years in Spain forever in the past.
Too late to wish that I had mastered Greek.
And all the etymologies amassed
within the single language I can speak
hold definitions disappearing fast
from common discourse. Many voices crowd
my ears, most often meaningless and loud.

Where shall I go with this polemic verse
composed outdoors in a grove of old white pines
towering above my head? Life could be worse,
and is, for most. Intelligence designs
vocabularies aimed to break the curse
of Babel, one true version that defines
the source that never can be spoken of:
hesed, amor, agape, logos, love.

Used

for S.L.G.

All shiny from the dealer's inventory,
its scars touched up, its tires and wipers new,
its flashy looks conceal a secret story.

The brilliant scarlet paint proclaims the glory
days of someone's youthful dream come true.
Found nowhere in the dealer's inventory:

the list of reasons someone had to worry
because the job got lost, the girlfriend, too,
her flashy looks a disappointing story,

the cold dispatch of every *I'm so sorry,*
depreciated hopes returning to
the showroom of some dealer's inventory.

What problems should we guess about before we
claim the shifts of fortune, points of view
assembled on four wheels, a future story,

before we're added to the category
of complicated things that people do,
this package from a dealer's inventory
that so conceals a long and secret story?

Ghazal

Even the stars in their misfortunes lie to me.
Never a kind spirit whispers its reply to me.

Lying awake in the dark, I can hear the river.
What solemn secrets its murmurings imply to me.

Holes in the night sky lurk, and suck the light in
like grave prowlers sinister and sly to me.

I am the lilac in your garden, a fragrant refuge.
See how the dithering sparrows fly to me.

From its perch up high, a focused hunger gazes
over the earth, turns its eagle eye to me.

Why do these songs pour out laments nightlong
in verses that so perfectly apply to me?

In a barbarian tongue, I call out again and again.
What comfort will your shuttered heart supply to me?

Watching the Poetry of the Deaf in ASL

I who hear selectively the voice
of my beloved from another room
am thinking now of those without a choice
to hear or not. And whether the living tomb
of silence gifts in them an element
of sense beyond my own, I can't presume.
When I consider how my life is spent
in words I play with in my mouth, my head,
awake, asleep, explaining what I meant,
then nothing could be worse for me to dread
than being shut away from all my toys
in a house where no one calls. I wish instead
to listen harder when my ear enjoys
the whole cacophony of human noise.

Poet Envy

Remember, darling, you are no one else.
That constant murmuring inside your head
pours out a stream of story no one tells
but you. And pretty soon when you are dead
you'll take it with you, going underground,
a dry bed where there was a river once.
For now, although you aim for sense in sound,
comparatively speaking, you're a dunce.

But never mind. The smallest seepings flow
together, unimagined and unseen,
and these white pines are sucking far below
to lift the darkness up alive and green.
And nothing is original or new
but you. There's ever only one of you.

At the Benedictine Abbey

The brothers file into accustomed places
after the bell for Vigils has been rung—
black robes, bald heads, assorted solemn faces,
stooped elderly, or licorice-thin and young.
The books before them open to the prayer
prescribed for them on this September day,
hours pulled across the planet everywhere
that monks are called from other work to pray.

Lives fitted to an ordered discipline
unfold as certain kinds of poetry
compress the passion of the soul within
and set on fire its full humanity.
The measure of the liturgy assured,
in silence comes the unexpected word.

Rondeau for Bill

The wind dies down. The moment you hoist sail,
another god determines to prevail
against the voyage you would undertake
across the lilting waters of the lake,
and makes both breezes and ambitions fail.

The air of afternoon goes still and stale.
A breath, a whiff, a zephyr would avail
the headway that your one-man boat could make.
The wind dies down.

Not that you'd want a hurricane or gale
to cause a tragic outcome of the tale.
And yet, how often fickle winds forsake
and never seem to give a guy a break.
A metaphor of undeserved betrayal,
the wind dies down.

A Momentary Stay

after R.F.

Morning pours out her gold,
melting over the cold
her treasury of light
that spills into the night
and banishes the stars,
Venus, Jupiter, and Mars
with uncorrupted day—
a momentary stay.

A Poem

Let it come to you quietly
      as sleep spilling
           into the lid of day.
Let it flow as naturally
      as rain running
           over the eaves of May.
Let it touch as tenderly
      as lovers' hands,
Be still
And easy as afternoon shadows
      sliding
           down a long hill.

III. What's so funny?

I don't want to make money. I just want to be wonderful.
—Marilyn Monroe

A Canadian Tragedy

Pierre, François, René
went out in a boat one day.

François, René, Pierre
felt raindrops in their hair.

A storm blew in. *Au revoir,*
René, Pierre, François.

Damnation!

In an email to faculty, Reehil wrote, "The curses and spells used in the books are actual curses and spells; which when read by a human being risk conjuring evil spirits into the presence of the person reading the text…"

Pastor Dan, of course you're vexed.
Harry Potter got us hexed.
Countless kids since '97
must have lost their shot at heaven,
doomed by conjured spirits' spell
to live forevermore in hell.
We understand that quite a few
past the age of twenty-two
are suffering from lost illusion,
burning in their souls' confusion.

Truth and fiction, fact and doubt,
faith and science, duke it out
and torture those who walk the brink
of finally learning how to think.
Evil kingdoms surely rule
when children are exposed at school
to random shootings, tv gore,
measles, dogmas, racist war,
standard tests, and even worse,
to ignorance: the damning curse.

The Roomba

Never watch a Roomba* if you want to keep your wits.
No chaos or uncertainty's more probable than its.

When loosed upon a room to clean the floor's entire expanse,
The Roomba, politician-wise, performs a crazy dance.

Its only wisdom is derived from bouncing off the walls,
Rebounding in whatever way the sensor first recalls,

And thus it never knows where it has been or what comes next
And seems to the observing mind perpetually perplexed.

It runs around in circles and it swerves both left and right,
Perhaps an indication that it isn't very bright.

Stymied in a corner or entangled in some fringes,
The Roomba halts completely and its inner world unhinges.

With bleats of incoherence it cries out for human hands
To lift it from the obstacles it never understands.

If you would drain a swamp or merely clean a dusty floor,
The aimless and unthinking are devices to ignore.

*a robotic vacuum

Beep

Shakespeare's time forever creeps
in petty pace, but our time beeps.
Beep. The stopwatch starts your run.
Beep. The coffee pot is done.
Beep. Beep. Beep. The timer's set.
Beep. The phone says *don't forget.*
Think of all the time we save
with beeps punched in the microwave.
Beeps that smoke alarms produce
demand a fresh supply of juice,
while one long beep, a distant cry,
declares your underwear is dry.
Beeps inform the copier
how many times to blink and blur,
(and bleating beeps mean Err…Err…Err…)
One beep sends annoyance through us:
Hold please. You're important to us.
Beeps with clumsy thumbs can make
a call to Iceland by mistake.
Miss a beep for someone's text?
Someone's likely to be vexed.
Beep. Your credit card is good.
Beep. Life's working as it should.
But let my fear be understood:
someday rescue me from science.
Please unplug me from reliance
on some medical appliance—
wired and tubed, deprived of sleep,
listening for that final…

Manhood

It starts at once. A little man
discovers that his little stream
shot upwards willy-nilly can
produce a corresponding scream.

The tender mom, the doting dad,
in spite of being rather pissed
will chuckle at the little lad,
his tummy will be rubbed and kissed,

and, handed round for show-and-tell
to beaming uncles, cooing aunts,
he learns he need not speak or spell.
The power's in his underpants.

And though some laurels he may win
for greater mind and braver heart,
the worthiness he feels within
will hang upon that single part.

Bleeping Bras

Jackson jail's screening policy on underwire bras causes an uproar.
Kansas City Star 6/4/19

Her underwires have caused a blip:
the lady lawyer has to strip.

What contraband might be holed up
suspiciously in that D-cup?

A shiv, a razor blade, a gun,
a six-pack, a forbidden phone?

A bra with such a sturdy frame
could hold a kilo of cocaine.

Attorneys wearing certain bras
are not exempted from the laws

preventing key and belt and shoe
and kitchen sink from passing through.

Never mind your background clearance.
There's no telling from appearance,

say officials, what's in there
besides your lacy underwear.

The hapless client's legal aid,
and justice, too, must be waylaid.

Stay-At-Home Improvement

The cat has a flapdoor for in-and-out going.
The gutters un-gummed keep the rainwater flowing.
The hinge that was squeaky?
The pipe that was leaky?
All fixed.
And that ratty old table? Antique-y!
The junk is hauled out
and the basement is clean.
A shim solves the shimmying
washing machine.
The driveway is sealed
from the house to the street.
The weeds in the grass
have gone down to defeat.
The porch swing is painted.
The sidewalk cemented.
The frenzied refurbishing?
Almost demented.
Have you been distraught, dear,
with nothing to do?
This buzzing and sawing
just isn't like you!
Devotion by demo?
I don't need the proof!
For godsake, my darling,
come down from the roof!

Opera: A Ballade

After watching 33 free streamed operas from the MET during quarantine

Sometimes the heroine is just a girl,
an innocent set up to be betrayed.
Whether she loves a hero or a churl,
she'll face a three- or four-hour escapade
in which her feelings and her fate are swayed
by charm, by force, deception, or disguise
she's helpless to resist or to evade.
And then she dies.

Sometimes around the heroine unfurl
fate's sinister entrapments. Undismayed,
she feels the storm of accusation swirl
and knows the price of honor must be paid.
Beset by Powers That Must Be Obeyed,
she suffers while the chorus vilifies.
Her hopes of justice and redemption fade.
And then she dies.

Sometimes the heroine, a perfect pearl,
whether a princess or a village maid,
regardless of her protest or demurral,
becomes the object of an evil trade,
a bloody game, a sinister charade,
with hidden motives and transparent lies,
with clash of insult and with flashing blade.
And then she dies.

Through every lamentation and tirade,
each heroine embraces her demise
despite how fervently she might have prayed.
And then…

Sitting in Church Behind the Beautiful Hair

The pew in front of me. I stare
directly at a mass of hair,
a hurly-burly chestnut hue
I wonder how a comb gets through.
The preacher's words, to get to me,
must dance around that pageantry
of gilded tresses. I'm enraptured
by that hair, enchanted, captured
by that hair I yearn to touch.
Was I once young and had so much?
A virgin claim no longer mine,
that flowing hair a maiden sign
like Cranach's Virgin peachy-sweet
demurely kneeled at Jesus' feet,
El Greco's Magdalene who shows
how golden-haired repentance flows,
or, lifted by a cherub horde,
Murillo's Mother of the Lord
with hair uncovered and unbound,
untouched in purity profound.
Must shave it off, some sects declare
who fear seduction of the hair.
Must cover it in public places.
While we're at it, *Veil their faces.*
Women, you must take the blame
for evil thoughts and sin and shame.
Yet rapt in hair, one solemn hour,
I'm wishing I could have that power.

*The works of art mentioned are on view at the Nelson-Atkins Museum of Art
Kansas City, Missouri.*

Old Proofreader Laments

It makes me see the color read
When I find lead instead of led.

I'm certain spellcheck doesn't care
when their is there instead of they're.

And plural's with apostrophes
are spreading like a dread disease,

meanwhile, a nouns possessive clout
is pitifully left without.

The language is confused, it's true,
by plough, enough, dough, thought, and through,

and yet I've pressed the classic rules
against the ignorance of fools.

My name in stone? I'll die well-versed.
(For godsake, check the spelling first.)

IV. Closing Remarks

Since then—'tis Centuries—and yet
Feels shorter than the Day
I first surmised the Horses' Heads
Were toward Eternity.
                    —Emily Dickinson

When the Rooms of My House Darken

I don't want to live where I can
see it coming: on a great plain
where the thundering mass
begins to spin, begins
to bear down on the fixed houses
and barns and towns.

When the rooms of my house darken
and the trees around me quiver, then
bend, and the sound of a train
I've been told about arrives, I
like everyone else have nowhere
to run and hide.

Three Rooms, Two Cats

The old man left her for a better place,
is how they used to say it. She moved, too
into the small, efficient sort of space
with just enough or not enough to do,
with her two cats, one friendly and one shy,
nowhere to wander and nowhere to hide.
Her own eternity of time rolls by,
and distant friends remark, *I thought she died.*

And so she does, but only by degrees.
Her creature comforts met, long life assured
by meds and meals and daily pleasantries,
she walks the corridors of death deferred,
forgotten, and forgetting everyone,
and every good she ever did undone.

At the Home

Old women curl like larvae
in the chrysalis of age
as though returning slowly
to an embryonic stage

and gradually excluded
from every human sense
await a resurrection
mysterious and immense.

Old Lady With No Complaints

The outward qualities already met:
the white hair, glasses, wrinkles, overweight,
the random names I'm likely to forget,
the words for things (like *icebox*) out of date.
The comfy sweats retirees get to wear?
I live in those, with *sneakers* on my feet.
Do I look puzzled with a distant stare
as though I needed help to cross the street?
I might be lost, but only lost in thought.
The road not taken troubles me no more.
Amused, I sift the clutter life has brought
and shut the past behind me door by door.
My bit in time seems infinitely small,
its prizes insufficient after all.

After the Eulogies

For D.S.

Out of the corner of my eye I see
a bald head passing, and I glance around.
Of course it isn't you. It couldn't be.
We've lately put your ashes in the ground.
But disbelief persists for quite a while.
Your presence, as before, behind the scene.
Back at the office, your unfailing smile.
Back in the kitchen, your *ad hoc* cuisine.

All of a sudden coming to the end,
you fell asleep and never saw the day.
Too soon, too young, we whisper friend to friend,
but rather wish we too might go that way.
So be remembered for your sidelong eyes,
your loving heart, and yes, your crazy ties.

Thank You For Your Service

after Siegfried Sassoon

You've made us proud--the prosperous and free.
It doesn't matter that a GED

was all the education you could get,
or that you signed up on a drunken bet.

It doesn't matter that the jobs are few
for unambitious, unskilled guys like you.

It doesn't matter you left bills to pay--
that girl and her two kids will be okay,

and you weren't ready yet to settle down.
What better way to kick that nothing town

and serve your country--or, at any rate,
some country you can't spell--to make ours great.

You vaguely knew from high school civics class
the Constitution would be worth your ass,

and there could be some glory in the flag,
adventure, and a lifelong chance to brag.

And so you took an oath and got a gun
and marched away to war that's never won.

It doesn't matter you saw children die
and never really knew the reasons why.

It doesn't matter that you left behind
your shattered heart, your shredded soul, your mind.

It doesn't matter nothing can restore
the same old nothing life you had before.

Virus Time

Walking I leave behind a plume of breath
invisible but loaded like a gun
that's pointed at the head of everyone
nearby. They wave at me and smile at death.

O neighborhood of much or little faith,
there's nothing novel underneath the sun
(all scriptures tell us) and no place to run.
We're looking evolution in the teeth.

What dull imagination would desire
apocalypse political and vague
arriving with the whimper of a plague
when we were promised meteoric fire?

Sometime After Today

Sometime after today, the snow will come
and fill this stand of cedar shoulder deep,
the cottage roof and woodpile weighted down,
the turtle buried in her winter sleep.

I have imagined coming here to see
the lake iced over, and the landscape changed
to a white canvas sketched in brown and green,
the shoreline shifted, landmarks rearranged,

no living sound, the solitude complete.
And would I love it then? I might discern
indifference whether I am here or not,
cold lesson I am hesitant to learn.

Sirens

On 39th Street, screaming east or west,
the sirens rip the air apart and make
a whorl of purpose, fading in their wake,
the destination sure, the fate unguessed.
Something gone wrong, an accident, a crime,
has summoned them, a heart attack or fire.
With help or hindrance as it may require,
the sirens strive to interfere in time.

Safe in my room, and startled out of sleep,
I can't prevent the circuits in my head
from spinning out scenarios of dread
and accusation—all the fear I keep
well-hidden—listening with the certainty
that sirens coming on will stop at me.

Closing the Cottage

We board the windows, cap the chimney, clean
the cupboards, bring the empty feeders in,
take final looks at the autumnal scene
before the shudders coming on begin.
A chilly sunlight dapples the afternoon
as we wrap up another island year.
We speak of how we came again in June,
anticipation not untinged with fear
of changes. But the cottage holds our place,
a bookmark in the stories of our lives
we can return to like a saving grace
of timelessness. Its history survives.
Yet these last tasks foreshadow what we grieve:
the only place we never have to leave.

V. Seasons

O World, I cannot hold thee close enough!
—Edna St. Vincent Millay

It is the Time to Listen

It is the time to listen. Things
Have begun to speak again
More wonderful than music, more
Articulate than men:
The animals who question
And stones that mourn.
Oh, who will translate for us these
Green tongues of corn?

At the Winter Solstice

Like veins and capillaries black
against the evening sky,
naked winter branches suck
the last hour dry.

As flesh of light diminishes,
so fades the blush of day,
until its colors vanish
into solemnity.

Playing With Fire

Crumpled headlines make the fiercest heat
for kindling. Only half-a-dozen days
will start you on a satisfying blaze
to torch this season's struggle and defeat.
Toss on a log. Repeat. Repeat. Repeat.
The structure shifts in unexpected ways.
Flame alternately surges and decays
as elements of earth and heaven meet.
Whatever burns you can incinerate:
yesterday's trash, old stories, and the names
you loved or hated going up in smoke
and sparks, or falling through the grate,
reduced to ash the universe reclaims.
You give the embers of your life a poke.

January

Far from the insect-busy summer day,
these engraved woods and fields lend
themselves to silence under snow suspended
windless against a ground of gray
and white. I've come to prefer the way
these small details, the leisurely agenda
of winter waiting for anything to happen,
give me less and less to say.

There are no other footprints where I walk
crunching like an awkward giant up the hill
until, in the full circle of the earth, I stop
for a while to listen, trying not to talk
even to myself. It is so still
I almost hear an owl's feather drop.

Matins

Small gray pinecones cluster on the bough
like little monks, each with a cap of sunlit sap.
A diamond gleams on every holy brow.

Pileated Woodpecker

Seldom I see her, but she can be heard:
red flamboyant headdress of a bird
banging her beak with quick intensity
against the instrument of a hollow tree.

Silence does not exist. Earth's made of sound,
her origins rumbling underneath the ground,
her surface an airy dance of blue-green grace
veiled in vibrations as she whirls in space.

Mornings I sit attempting to achieve
one-ness with the silence that I disbelieve
fill with the hum and whir of wind and wings,
woodpeckers, and other transitory things.

The Moth

With my paddle, I lifted from the calm
surface of the water
a brown moth the size of my palm,

each of its top wings spotted
with a deceiving eye, its fuzzy thumb
of a body daintily mottled.

I laid it, to carry it home
dead, I thought, on the kayak bow.
Then it began to tremble.

Sign of reviving life, or final throe?
I decided to set it out on the nearest shore
to live again or die, I'll never know,

or what untimely hazard breezes tore
those ragged wings I left in the sun to dry.

Prairie

Where I come from there are waves of taffeta
as deep as summer and
as silent as the spaces between
stones. All day and night
I do not hear them crashing. Those waves
are full of peace, oh, like the dress
one may put on to drown in: grass
alive and sensuous, a gown as big as god
to fold around you and lie down in
to be born.

Forecast

very strong probability
instruments which measure
based on previous
virtually no possibility
the unlikely event
under similar conditions
only slight indications
often happens when
50% chance
be prepared for
changed from earlier
currently out there
though not unexpected
some signs suggesting
perhaps by tomorrow

Stars

Upon its tilted spindle
       the bowl of heaven turns
with starry illustrations of
       the tales on Grecian urns.
There Perseus, Andromeda, and
       Hercules roll by,
as though some everlasting truth
       were written in the sky.

Imagine all the languages
       the universe can speak
to those who never heard or read
       or thought a word of Greek:
bone auguries from China, and
       the handprints in a cave,
the calendar of Yucatan,
       and runes that mark a grave.

From drums of Africa, and winds
       upon Pacific seas,
from mathematic measure,
       and the atom's mysteries
receive the wisdom of the earth
       in wordless seminars
assembled by the human mind
       from dust that once was stars.

The Impressionist

The day emerges from the morning mist
like thought that slowly, slowly takes on form.
The lake like ancient silver, amethyst
the sky before the sun, after the storm
a calm, and the bell-like call of a shy bird.
See how gold flows down over the trees
until the shapes and colors softly blurred
assume their proper detail by degrees.

The earth has been itself without my eyes,
my ears to hear, or mind imagining
the way it came to be, and I surmise
will be itself tomorrow. Everything
unspoken will eventually be said
in stone layers heavy above my head.

About the Author

Hundreds of verses into her career as a writer for Hallmark Cards, Barbara Loots remained essentially anonymous. However, her optimistic view of life surely touched thousands of lives with a broad swath of social communications, from birthdays to holidays to care of the grieving. She is the author of a number of children's books published by Hallmark. She retired after forty-one years.

Meanwhile, her work as a poet has been appearing in print since the 1960s in magazines such as *The Lyric, Blue Unicorn, New Letters, Measure, Cricket,* and *The Christian Century.* Anthologies include *The Random House Treasury of Light Verse, The Helicon Nine Reader, The Muse Strikes Back, The Whirlybird Anthology of Kansas City Writers, Landscapes With Women,* and *Love Affairs at the Villa Nelle.* Online, her poems appear in *Better Than Starbucks, Mezzo Cammin, The Ekphrastic Review,* and *Light Poetry Magazine,* among others.

In 2014, her collection *Road Trip* was published by Kelsay Books/White Violet Press. Her second collection, *Windshift,* also published by Kelsay Books, received third place for the 2019 Thorpe Menn Award for Literary Excellence. Individual poems have won recognition in various literary magazines.

She resides in Kansas City, Missouri, where she volunteers as a Docent for the renowned Nelson-Atkins Museum of Art and worships with the Presbyterians at Second Church. She is married to Bill Dickinson, and obeys orders from Bob the Cat.

Author's blog: barbaraloots.com

Other poetry collections by this author:

Road Trip

Windshift

Available from Kelsaybooks.com or amazon.com

Made in the USA
Monee, IL
25 October 2020

46039975R00046